Table of Contents

Preface

This eBook describes the Ansoff Matrix, a strategic planning tool that links an organization's marketing strategy with its general strategic direction.

You will learn:

- How the Ansoff Matrix can help you to develop a strategy for improving your market position
- The four ways that an increase in market penetration can be achieved
- The risks inherent in a market development strategy and how these can be minimized
- The three approaches to brand extension that can maximize the opportunities for success whilst minimizing the risks
- The three methods that organizations can use to diversify into new markets with new products

Introduction

Today's organizations find themselves operating in an environment that is changing faster than ever before. The process of analyzing the implications of these changes and modifying the way that the organization reacts to them is known as business strategy.

> 'Strategy is the direction and scope of an organization over the long term, which achieves advantage in a changing environment through its configuration of resources and competences' Johnson et al. (2008).

While your role as a manager is unlikely to require you to make decisions at the strategic level, you may be asked to contribute your expertise to meetings where strategic concerns are being discussed. You may also be asked to comment on pilot schemes, presentations, reports, or statistics that will affect future strategy.

Whether you work in a large multinational corporation or a small organization, a good understanding of the appropriate business analysis techniques and terminology will help you to contribute to the strategic decision—making processes.

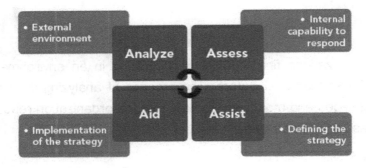

Typical scenarios where you could be asked to provide information and data for your organization's strategic decision making include:

- Analyzing the organization's external environment.

- Assessing the organization's internal capabilities and how well it can respond to external forces.

- Assisting with the definition of the organization's strategy.

- Aiding in the implementation of the organization's strategy.

The diagram above shows where five widely used business analysis tools fit into the strategic planning process. This series of eBooks will give you a solid understanding of how these tools can be used, as well as an appreciation of their limitations.

This knowledge will enable you to take an active and productive role when asked to participate in the strategic decision—making process.

KEY POINTS

✓ You may be asked to contribute your expertise to meetings where strategic concerns are being discussed.

✓ Typical scenarios where you could be asked to provide information for strategic decision making include: analyzing the organization's external environment, assessing internal capabilities, assisting strategy definitions, and aiding in the implementation.

Ansoff Matrix

The Ansoff Matrix, or Ansoff Box, is a business analysis technique that provides a framework enabling growth opportunities to be identified. It can help you consider the implications of growing the business through existing or new products and in existing or new markets. Each of these growth options draws on both internal and external influences, investigations, and analysis that are then worked into alternative strategies.

Prior to using the Ansoff Matrix your organization should conduct a SWOT analysis. This technique is described in detail in the 'SWOT Analysis' eBook, which can be downloaded from www.free-management-ebooks.com.

The SWOT analysis serves to identify the strengths and weaknesses of your organization, as well as the external threats to it and the opportunities available to it. Once these have been identified you can use the Ansoff Matrix to investigate the implications of your organization's current strategy and those of any changes that are suggested by the SWOT analysis.

The usefulness of both the SWOT analysis and Ansoff Matrix depends on the quality and accuracy of the market intelligence they are based on. This information is best supplied by working managers who can provide accurate and up — to—date information on everything from customer feedback to competitor activities.

The need for this information means that you may find yourself in strategy meetings; a familiarity with the underlying business analysis techniques and jargon can help you to make a valuable contribution by bringing your own area of expertise into the discussion.

The Ansoff Matrix, created by the American planning expert Igor Ansoff, is a strategic planning tool that links an organization's marketing strategy with its general strategic direction. It presents four alternative growth strategies in the form of a 2x2 table or matrix.

One dimension of the matrix considers 'products' (existing and new) and the other dimension considers 'markets' (existing and new).

Products

	Existing	New
Existing	Market Penetration	Product Development
New	Market Development	Diversification

Markets

The resulting matrix offers a structured way to assess potential strategies for growth. As part of this framework you will have to consider possible technological advances that could affect your current and future products, as well as potentially new markets for both sets of products during their life cycle.

The sequence of these strategies is:

1. **Market Penetration**—You focus on selling your existing products or services to your existing markets to achieve growth in market share.

2. **Market Development**—You focus on developing new markets or market segments for your existing products or services.

3. **Product Development**—You focus on developing new products or services for your existing markets.

4. **Diversification**—You focus on the development of new products to sell into new markets.

The matrix does not present you with a final decision as to whether or not to develop new products or enter new markets, but it does provide you with an outline of alternative methods by which you can achieve your mission or growth targets.

It is particularly useful in showing how you can develop a strategy for altering your market position as well as increasing or improving your product range. The four different options are not mutually exclusive and in certain circumstances your organization might want to combine different elements.

The output from an Ansoff Matrix is a series of suggested growth strategies that serve to set the direction for the business and provide marketing strategies to achieve them.

Each of these options carries a certain amount of risk and involves differing levels of investment.

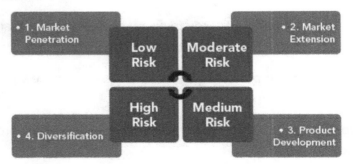

To be able to take an active part in discussions regarding any one of these four strategies requires you to have a general idea of the implications each strategy could have on your organization.

KEY POINTS

- ✔ The Ansoff Matrix is a strategic planning tool that links an organization's marketing strategy with its general strategic direction.

- ✔ Prior to using the Ansoff Matrix your organization should conduct a SWOT analysis.

- ✔ One dimension of the matrix considers 'products' (existing and new) and the other dimension considers 'markets' (existing and new).

- ✔ This suggests four possible strategies: Market Penetration, Market Development, Product Development, and Diversification.

Market Penetration Strategy

This strategy involves focusing on selling your existing products or services into your existing markets to gain a higher market share. This is the first strategy most organizations will consider because it carries the lowest amount of risk.

This strategy involves selling more to current customers and to new customers who can be thought of as being in the same marketplace. For example, if your current customer base consists of men aged between 16 and 25 then this strategy would involve attempting to sell more of your existing products or services to this same group.

One key constraint is that you cannot allow anything in your drive to grow market share to compromise your existing success. You need to be aware of what has made the product a success so far and ensure that nothing you do will undermine it.

You should give this strategy careful consideration if you are not in a position to invest heavily or are not comfortable with taking risks, as the amount of risk associated with this strategy is relatively low.

There are four approaches you can adopt when implementing this strategy:

Market Penetration Strategy:
- Retain or increase your product's market share
- Dominate growth markets
- Drive out your competitors
- Increase existing customer usage

Maintain or increase the market share of current products

You can achieve this by adopting a strategy that is made up of a combination of competitive pricing strategies, advertising, and sales promotion. This would involve focusing on the areas of sales and marketing responsible for managing the pricing and promotion of the product.

Secure dominance of growth markets

Another approach you could take is identify a new demographic for your product, for example another age group. An excellent example of such a strategy would be for you to identify a change in the age distribution of your product users and to then aggressively market your product to this age group.

This was exactly what happened in the cell phone market when it was realized that teenagers were emerging as a key demographic. Previously it had been users in their 20s who were seen as the biggest group of first — time users. Substantial growth in market share and dominance in this sector was achieved by ensuring cell phone companies' promotions met the needs of this younger group.

Your role in the discussion senior executives will have in defining their strategy is that of providing the market intelligence or customer feedback that helps to inform the executive team of the current dynamics of the market. The data you provide will help the team decide whether a growth market is an extension of the current market or is truly a 'new' market. This decision is likely to be based on how your organization is going to approach this growth market.

If the team's chosen approach defines the growth market as a 'new' one then a market penetration strategy will be replaced with one of market development, which is covered in the next section.

Restructure a mature market by driving out competitors

Many organizations find themselves in a mature or saturated market and to achieve further market share requires a different approach. This strategy requires an aggressive promotional campaign, supported by a pricing strategy designed to make the market unattractive for smaller competitors.

With a mature market there are no more demographic sectors to exploit and the only way to attain market share is to take it from competitors. Examples of this strategy can be seen in the newspaper, telecoms, and cable TV industries, where the larger players now dominate. Another good example is the rapid growth of the supermarket chains, which have taken market share from small high street grocers who are unable to compete on price and product range. More recently there has been the introduction of loyalty campaigns, where the supermarkets compete for market share through customer loyalty programs.

Increase usage by existing customers

Another approach to market penetration is to persuade your existing customers to use your product or service more frequently. There are several tactics you could use to do this, including loyalty schemes, adding value to the current product, or making alterations to the product that encourage greater use.

The tactics of this approach all aim to 'tie in' your customers to your product or service by making it more difficult for them to move to another supplier. The ability of your organization to achieve higher usage by customers can be greatly enhanced by rapidly changing technologies that encourage users to upgrade or that offer more reasons to use the product or service. A good example of this would be cell phones: models are now upgraded every six to 12 months with the addition of new features and capabilities.

A successful market penetration strategy relies on detailed knowledge of the market and competitor activities. It relies on you having successful products in a market that you already know well.

The key role you are likely to be asked to perform is capturing the intelligence that is required to make informed decisions. Understanding why this information is being asked for should help you to capture and pass on the most relevant and significant information.

KEY POINTS

- ✔ Market penetration involves focusing on selling your existing products or services into your existing markets to gain a higher market share.

- ✔ This can be achieved in four ways: maintaining or increasing the market share of current products; securing dominance of growth markets; restructuring a mature market by driving out competitors; or increasing usage by existing customers.

Market Development Strategy

A market development strategy involves selling your existing products into new markets. There are a variety of ways that this strategy can be achieved.

New geographical markets

This could involve expanding outside of your region or selling to a new country or a new continent. The element of risk in adopting this strategy will depend on whether or not you can use your established sales channels in the new market.

New product dimensions or packaging

Your organization may simply want to repackage your product so that it can open up a whole new market. For example, a company that sold industrial cleaning products in 20 — liter containers could break into the domestic market by repackaging in smaller quantities and developing a suitable brand image.

If you are responsible for packaging or production of the product you will be required to look at the new costs involved with these changes and new markets requirements and alter the marketing messages so that they are appropriate to that country's culture.

New distribution channels

Many companies have transformed themselves from high street retailers into

Internet retailers. As a manager you could be expected to outline the internal and financial implications of such a change. Senior management would be looking for you to provide the details of how to make this approach a success.

This could include the training needs of employees so that they have the skills to fulfill Internet orders, whether they are taking incoming calls or processing online orders. You would need to demonstrate an understanding of the operational changes your organization would face, such as a centralized warehouse rather than local depots.

One example of this type of market development is the sale of high — end sports equipment, which is now almost exclusively sold online rather than through sports equipment retailers. Another example is the sale of DVDs in retail outlets like supermarkets and gas stations rather than specialist entertainment stores selling predominantly music and video products.

Different pricing policies to create a new market segment

The important aspect of this approach is whether or not current users can easily alter their purchases to take advantage of the new market pricing. A good example of how to protect your existing market whilst developing a new one is Adobe Photoshop. It protected its price difference of hundreds of dollars of its original professional product by offering a reduced 'home' version that had a restricted set of functions.

Whilst there are similarities between the first two strategies, market development involves a greater degree of uncertainty, risk, and financial commitment.

One of the biggest dangers of this strategy is the risk of alienating your current customers. For example, the tools made by US company Snap — on are widely regarded as the best in the world and are used by almost all professional automotive racing teams.

Snap — on tools are only available through a tightly controlled network of franchisees and the company has resisted the temptation to develop any markets outside of professional mechanics. This strategy has allowed Snap — on to maintain its position as the number one supplier in this highly competitive market.

One way around this problem is to sell a cheaper product under a different sub — brand. This is something that has been done successfully by the US musical instrument company Fender, which created the 'Squier' sub — brand in order to market budget instruments without alienating its core market of musicians who want to own a recognizably highend instrument.

KEY POINTS

✔ A market development strategy involves selling your existing products into new markets.

✔ There are four strategies that can achieve this: new geographical markets; new product dimensions or packaging; new distribution channels; or the creation of a new market segment by means of different pricing.

✔ One of the biggest dangers of this strategy is the risk of alienating your current customers.

Product Development Strategy

This growth strategy requires changes in business operations, including a research and development (R&D) function that is needed to introduce new products to your existing customer base.

As part of a successful product development strategy your role will require you to have a greater appreciation of a new emphasis placed on marketing. This would result in you supplying data for and assessing the implications of change in the following key areas:

Research and development

You may find yourself having to investigate and assess the use of new technologies, processes, and materials that would be needed to pursue this strategy.

In the cell phone market, for example, phone models are being replaced every six months or so. Your organization may find that the lifespan of its products are longer, but few can ignore the necessity of continuous R&D.

Assessing customer needs

This is something that can be done by the marketing department in the form of customer questionnaires and user groups. However, customer needs can also be become apparent to people who are in customer — facing roles, as they often are the first to hear about problems or concerns with the product or service.

f you are managing a team in a customer — facing role you will have the opportunity to gather data that may initially appear negative but which can offer your organization the opportunity to meet customers' needs more fully. Understanding what a customer's real needs are and how these can be interpreted in product development is essential to success when using this strategy.

For example, complaints about oil spilling over the customer's car engine when having to replace lost oil led to the addition of an integral funnel being added to engine oil packaging.

Brand extension

This is a common method of launching a new product by using an existing brand name on a new product in a different category. A company using brand extension hopes to leverage its existing customer base and brand loyalty. However, this is a high — risk strategy as success is impossible to predict and if a brand extension is unsuccessful, it can harm the parent brand. Common sense would suggest that for brand extension to be successful there should be some logical association between the original product and the new one, but there have been many exceptions to this.

It is extremely difficult to predict what will work and what will not, and even with the benefit of hindsight it is sometimes hard to see why some attempts at brand extension succeed whilst others fail. For example:

A well — known success is the launch of a clothing range by Caterpillar, a company that makes earth — moving equipment. This brand extension is totally unrelated to its main business.

A well—known failure is that of the car manufacturer Volvo, whose launch of its 850 GLT sports sedan was a high—profile failure. This seemed on the surface to be a logical brand extension, but it did not work for Volvo because the public could not be persuaded to buy a sports car from a manufacturer whose principal brand value is safety.

Whatever course of action is decided upon it must not create confusion amongst your customers. It must also avoid having a detrimental effect on your current market share.

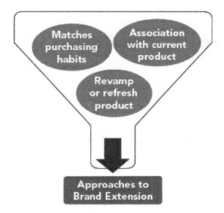

There are three broad approaches to new product development:

1. The new product is closely associated with current products.

2. The new product matches current customers' purchasing habits.

3. The new product reinvents or refreshes the existing product.

Within the fast moving consumer goods (FMCGs) market the majority of product development follows the first approach of creating new products that are easily and closely associated with the existing product. These new products usually have strong brand awareness within the market and use this as their main vehicle to gain visibility in this highly competitive market.

For example:

Mars is well known for its famous Mars snack bar. Its brand extension remained in the snack arena and started with different sizes, such as bite size and king size. Then it created a branded ice cream before moving into beverages.

Kit Kat's product development has been similar to that of Mars, but it has tried offering customers different flavors as part of this strategy. This has met with varying degrees of success. The United Kingdom has shown little preference for the new flavors, whereas in Japan flavors such as Wasabi, pumpkin, and toasted soy flour have become very popular.

Kit Kat's variable success with creating new favors for their chocolate bars reflects how different cultural tastes can influence success or failure when using this strategy. If your organization operates internationally then part of your research and development should take account of cultural differences.

The second brand extension approach requires your organization to have a thorough knowledge of the purchasing habits of your existing customers. Using this expertise you would then develop your products in such a way that they match these habits.

You may even exploit your organization's or your brand's image and reputation to achieve this by promoting and mirroring your existing brand image and its purchasing habits onto your new product.

For example:

> Marks & Spencer used their image of quality to expand their product range into food, encouraging their existing customers to buy from them rather than a supermarket. They have also extended their brand into financial services.

> Virgin exploited their image of quality and offering something more exciting to persuade teenagers and young adults who bought music from them to buy soft drinks (Virgin cola), travel with them, and later to use their banking services and other financial products.

The third approach to brand extension is to continuously offer a refreshed or revamped product. This new product must convert your competitor's customers rather than simply cannibalizing your own sales. You want to avoid diverting your existing sales to the new product as this will simply maintain revenues rather than increase your market share.

Razors, washing detergent, and cars are all examples of products that are continually 'refreshed' in this way, especially to stay distinct from the competition and gain market share.

For example:

> The washing detergents market has seen extensive product development. Companies started offering just one type of washing powder; this then progressed to one for

whites and another for colors, then to liquid versions, and now to tabs or pouches.

The consumer will buy a variety of these products to satisfy the different washing requirements of their clothes. This contrasts with previous generations who just used one powder to wash everything!

Each of these product development approaches involves investment and an element of risk. One key aspect of this strategy is that you as a manager are likely to have to develop new skills and specializations within your team or department to meet these new requirements.

These new skills, especially in the initial stages, could be met by using outside skills and resources to control the cost and risk of such a venture. Many organizations outsource this aspect of product development and simply add their name to the packaging.

Product development, especially brand extension, is a popular strategy because it is more easily accomplished within the organization than creating totally new products.

KEY POINTS

- ✔ A product development strategy involves developing new products or services for your existing markets.

- ✔ This strategy requires continuous research & development as well as the ongoing assessment of customer needs.

- ✔ There are three broad approaches: the new product is closely associated with current products; it matches current customers' purchasing habits; or it reinvents or refreshes the existing product.

- ✔ Many organizations outsource product development by simply buying in an existing product from another manufacturer and putting their own name on the packaging.

Diversification Strategy

A diversification strategy achieves growth by developing new products for completely new markets. As such, it is inherently more risky than product development because by definition the organization has little or no experience of the new market. In addition, the new skills needed both in terms of marketing and operations often require substantial investment. This is usually achieved by acquiring an organization already operating in the new market.

For an organization to adopt such a strategy it must have a clear idea of what it expects to gain in terms of its growth. It also needs to make an honest assessment of the risks involved. Diversification often fails because organizations that attempt it are doing so because they have uncompetitive products in shrinking markets and a diversification strategy represents a desperate attempt to reinvent themselves. However, for those organizations that find the right balance between risk and reward, a marketing strategy of diversification can be highly rewarding.

This strategy is unlikely to come as a surprise to you, as it will have been intimated in many executive discussions and communications as a way the organization can achieve its ambitious or aggressive growth targets.

By regularly reading press articles on your organization and its annual report you will be able to ascertain if this type of strategy is one under consideration. If you are aware of the accumulation of investment funds or substantial pressures from your competitors on your market share or product range, then these are the type of pre—conditions that forewarn of a diversification strategy.

If you are involved in defining or implementing a diversification strategy you will be aware of the discomfort or risk that occurs when working outside your existing knowledge base. Not all such strategies are successful, and even those that are in the short term may falter in the long run if they are unable to match the R&D of their competitors.

These two examples illustrate the risks involved:

In the UK, Virgin's move into trains has not been as successful as was initially hoped, even though they had some experience in the transport market. This poor performance might have had an impact on the overall strength of the brand due to the criticisms of the rail service. But Richard Branson's image has done much to minimize the impact and enhance the corporation's ability to truly segment its services.

Nokia were extremely successful when they diversified into cell phone manufacturing from their original focus as a producer of paper products. They became the European market leader, but they have recently suffered a setback with the introduction of Smartphones. It will take them time to respond to this setback and restore their market position.

Diversification can occur at two levels: either at the business unit level or at an organizational level. When it happens at the business unit level, you will most likely see your organization expanding into a new segment of its current market. At the organizational level, you will most likely find you are involved in integrating a new organization into your existing one.

As with each of the other growth strategies there are three broad approaches to how your organization implements a policy of diversification:

- Full Diversification
- Backward Diversification
- Forward Diversification

Some organizations refer to these types of diversification as different 'integration' approaches because this is actually what happens. The new product or service and its market must be 'integrated' into the organizational structure to be successful.

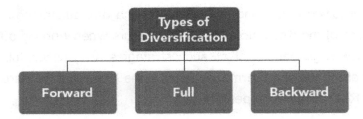

Full Diversification—this approach is the most risky as you are offering a totally new product or service to an unknown market. It will also take considerable time to accomplish. An example of this strategy would be:

A fresh trout distributor decides to diversify into selling insurance.

Backward diversification—this is where your organization decides to diversify by offering a product or service that relates to the preceding stage of your current product or service. For example:

The distributor decides to invest in a Scottish trout farm, thereby encroaching on the role of his or her supplier.

Forward diversification—this is the situation where your organization diversifies into the products or services that relate to a later stage that follows your current offering. For example:

The distributor negotiates contracts directly with the supermarkets and other end users by selling online, negating the need to work with wholesalers.

In each of these examples the distributor would need to learn new skills and methods of operation. In the examples of forward and backward diversification those skills are not so alien to the distributor because the product is essentially the same. But the expertise in running a trout farm, in negotiating contracts, and setting up a reliable online shop to the public will require new skills to be successful.

In this example, the option of full diversification is obviously very risky indeed.

The distributor is not involved in the insurance business and few of the skills that exist within his or her existing business will be transferable to the new one. This type of radical diversification can work if the company is cash rich and feels as though they would benefit from investing in a completely different type of business, perhaps one that they believe has a better long—term future than their current enterprise.

KEY POINTS

- ✔ A diversification strategy achieves growth by developing new products for completely new markets.

- ✔ Diversification can occur at two levels: either at the business unit level or at an organizational level.

- ✔ The three approaches to diversification or integration are: full diversification, backward diversification, and forward diversification.

Summary

The Ansoff Matrix can be used to explore the different directions for strategic growth that a company might take. The output from the matrix is a series of suggested growth strategies that serve to set the direction for the business strategy. Each of these options carries a certain amount of risk and involves some investment.

The matrix was designed for use by established organizations that have the financial security to pursue the chosen strategy. It is not designed to be used by failing organizations that are trying to reinvent themselves just to survive.

Other business strategy eBooks available from www.free-management-ebooks.com include:

- SWOT Analysis
- Boston Box
- PESTLE Analysis
- Porter's Five Forces

www.ingramcontent.com/pod-product-compliance
Lightning Source LLC
Chambersburg PA
CBHW070929050326
40689CB00015B/3679